Hea

Protein

Nancy Dickmann

Chicago, Illinois

www.capstonepub.com
Visit our website to find out more information about Heinemann-Raintree books.

To order:

☎ Phone 888-454-2279

🖳 Visit www.capstonepub.com to browse our catalog and order online.

Edited by Rebecca Rissman and Adrian Vigliano
Designed by Joanna Hinton-Malivoire
Picture research by Elizabeth Alexander
Production by Victoria Fitzgerald
Originated by Capstone Global Library Ltd
Printed in the United States of America by Worzalla Publishing.

15 14 13 12 11
10 9 8 7 6 5 4 3 2 1

Library of Congress Cataloging-in-Publication Data
Cataloging-in-Publication data is on file at the Library of Congress.

ISBN 978-1-4329-6976-9 (hc) -- ISBN 978-1-4329-6983-7 (pb)

Acknowledgments
We would like to thank the following for permission to reproduce photographs: © Capstone Publishers pp.5, 12, 14, 22 (Karon Dubke); Corbis p.13 (© Image Source); Getty Images pp.4 (Kevin Summers/Photographer's Choice), 10 (Inga Spence/Visuals Unlimited), 11 (Dorling Kindersley), 21 (Jon Feingersh/Iconica); iStockphoto pp.8 (© Ronald Fernandez), 23 top (© Mark Hatfield); Photolibrary pp.7 (Jo Whitworth/Garden Picture Library), 9 (Animals Animals/Robert Maier), 20 (Peter Mason/Cultura); Shutterstock pp.6 (© BESTWEB), 15, 23 middle (© Juriah Mosin), 16 (© a9photo), 17, 23 bottom (© Joe Gough), 18 (© Monkey Business Images); U.S. Department of Agriculture, Center for Nutrition Policy and Promotion p.19.

Front cover photograph of meat, fish, eggs, nuts, and beans reproduced with permission of © Capstone Publishers (Karon Dubke). Back cover photograph of fish reproduced with permission of iStockphoto (© Ronald Fernandez).

Every effort has been made to contact copyright holders of material reproduced in this book. Any omissions will be rectified in subsequent printings if notice is given to the publishers.

Contents

Meat, Fish, Eggs, Beans, and Nuts

Meat and beans are foods that we eat.

We also eat fish, eggs, and nuts.

Meat comes from animals such as cows.

Beans come from plants.

tuna

Fish comes from animals such as tuna.

Eggs come from birds such
as chickens.

Nuts grow on trees.

Eating these foods can keep us healthy.

Helping Your Body

Meat, fish, eggs, beans, and nuts all have protein.

You need protein to grow.

Eating beans gives you energy.

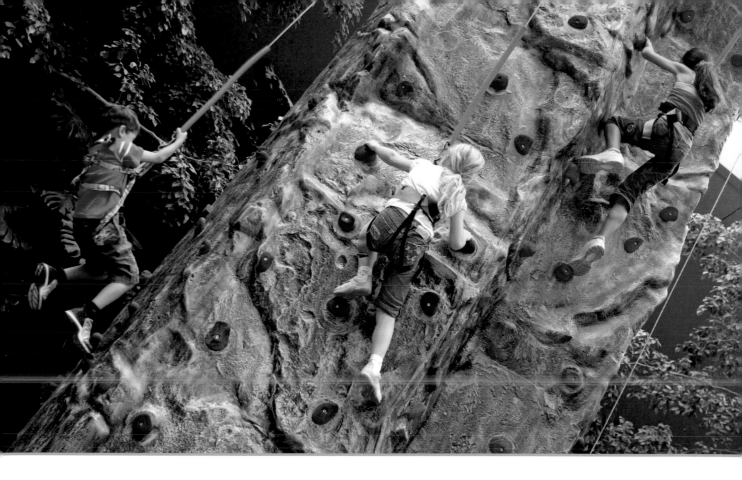

You need energy to work and play.

fish

Eating lean meat and fish helps keep your blood healthy.

Some meat has a lot of fat. Too much fat can hurt your body.

Healthy Eating

We need to eat different kinds of food each day.

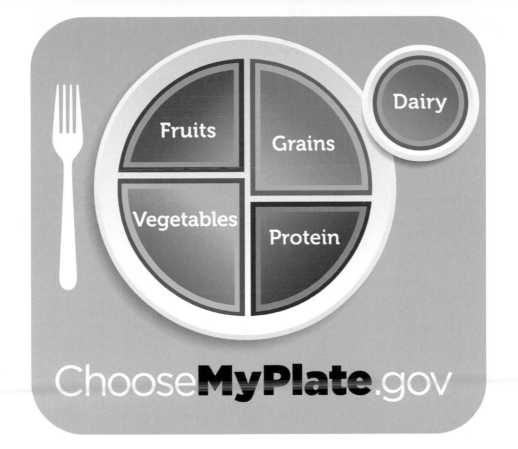

MyPlate reminds us to eat some foods from each food group every day.

We eat lean meat and other protein foods to stay healthy.

We eat these foods because they taste good!

Find the Meat

Here is a healthy dinner. Can you find a food made from meat?

Answer on page 24

Picture Glossary

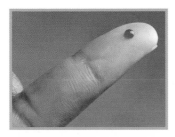 **blood** red liquid inside your body. Blood takes food and air to all your body parts.

 **energy** the power to do something. We need energy when we work or play.

 **fat** oily thing in some foods. Your body uses fat to keep warm. Eating too much fat is bad for your body.

Index

Answer to quiz on page 22: The meat food is chicken.

Notes for parents and teachers

Before reading

Explain that we need to eat a range of different foods to stay healthy. Introduce the protein element of the MyPlate graphic on page 19. Our bodies use protein to help build many of our body parts, including our skin, hair, muscles, bones, and blood. Protein helps our bodies grow.

After reading

- Discuss the fact that some people do not eat meat and fish (vegetarians) and some do not eat meat, fish, eggs, or dairy (vegans). Brainstorm other foods they can eat to make sure they get enough protein.

- Explain that some people do not eat certain types of meat, or only eat meat that has been prepared in a certain way because of their religious beliefs. Buddhist: no meat or fish; Hindu: no beef; Jewish: Kosher meat, no pork or shellfish; Muslim: Halal meat, no pork; Sikh: no pork or beef. Share experiences of this as a class.